# OUTSTANDING

## P o c

Caroline
Bentley-Davies

Superb ✓
Excellent ✓
Magnificent ✓
Brilliant ✓
Cool! ✓

Cartoons:
Phil Hailstone

Published by:

**Teachers' Pocketbooks**
Laurel House, Station Approach,
Alresford, Hampshire SO24 9JH, UK
Tel: +44 (0)1962 735573
Fax: +44 (0)1962 733637
Email: sales@teacherspocketbooks.co.uk
Website: www.teacherspocketbooks.co.uk

*Teachers' Pocketbooks is an imprint of
Management Pocketbooks Ltd.*

Series editor – Linda Edge.

With thanks to Brin Best for his help in
launching the series.

© Caroline Bentley-Davies 2011

This edition published 2011. Reprinted 2012.
ISBN: 978 1 906610 35 7

E-book ISBN: 978 1 908284 83 9

British Library Cataloguing-in-Publication
Data – A catalogue record for this book is
available from the British Library.

Design, typesetting and graphics by **Efex Ltd**.
Printed in UK.

# Contents

# Foreword

Teaching outstanding lessons is an aspiration that all teachers share. We all want to know what to do to make our lessons highly successful because when we teach great lessons we have better motivated, engaged and interested students. These are young people who will not only fulfil their potential in examinations and wider life skills, but who will enjoy and remember what they have been taught.

In the UK, Ofsted rates the best lessons as '*outstanding*' and many teachers clamour to know how to deliver one of these lessons. But being a great teacher isn't about pulling the occasional 'perfect' lesson out of the bag for an observation or inspection; it is about developing excellent relationships with pupils and honing our skills and judgements about them on a daily basis. This is what enables us to teach great lessons consistently – rather than feeling they are huge theatrical productions that can only be arranged and ordered well in advance with plenty of effort and props!

# Foreword

Even the best teachers have lessons that don't quite hit the mark. However, they don't let the occasional setback or failure deter them. Excellent teachers know how important it is to set themselves high expectations, even if they occasionally fall short in delivery.

They learn by trying things out and reflecting on what was successful and what was less so. Great lessons are built from adapting and improving on an aspect of a lesson that did not go quite as well as planned.

Pupils appreciate the efforts of a teacher who sets high standards. The attitude you adopt towards your own teaching practice will be picked up on consciously and subconsciously by the pupils you teach. Raising your game will help them to raise theirs.

'The greater danger for most of us lies not in setting our aim too high and falling short; but in setting our aim too low, and hitting the mark.'
**Michelangelo**

# Foreword

The tips in this Pocketbook will enable you to develop the skills to teach a stunning lesson, one that will knock the socks off your observer, but the book has a much broader remit. In looking at developing outstanding lessons, it considers crucial factors drawn from current classroom practice, educational research, and pupil feedback.

As you read, bear in mind that the success of any lesson will be determined by how you respond and tailor your teaching to your class's changing reactions. How are they finding the lesson? How are they tackling the work? What does their feedback tell you?

This book isn't a simple checklist of everything that makes a 'perfect' lesson. Teaching isn't that straightforward and thank goodness for that! What you *will* find are the key things to consider when planning and teaching your lessons and a range of practical classroom strategies and suggestions. Think about them, sift and select, trial them, and most importantly **adapt** them to meet *your* pupils' needs.

So, are you ready to give it a go?

Myth vs
Reality

 Developing
Great
Relationships

 Planning
Outstanding
Lessons

 It's About
Them – Not
You!

The X Factor

 Resources
and
Techniques

 Motivate
'em!

 Moving
Forward

# M y t h   v s   R e a l i t y

# Misconceptions

The key factor in determining whether a lesson is outstanding is how well the pupils are learning and whether they are making excellent progress. What does the teacher do to engage, motivate and challenge their students? What impact does the lesson have on them?

Some teachers feel that there are lots of seemingly impossible ingredients required to teach an outstanding lesson. Common misconceptions include:

- Always having to write up lesson objectives at the start of the lesson
- Always reviewing the learning at the end of the lesson
- Always having to use ICT
- Ensuring that peer and self-assessment are part of each and every lesson
- Using teaching techniques that relate to visual, auditory and kinaesthetic learners in *every* lesson
- Having perfectly behaved pupils, or pupils working in silence 100% of the time

In all of these instances the rule is the same: the focus needs to be on **the relevance of the activities and how they contribute towards pupils' learning**.

# Some myths

Let's unpick a few myths about the 'perfect lesson'. Doing so, will help us explore some key elements in outstanding lessons:

**Myth 1.** *'The teacher does all of the work'.*

**Reality** – It's the pupils who should be working hardest in the lesson – not you! We all know that if somebody just tells us how to do something we rarely remember it. It is by being active in our own learning, whether through discussion, note-making, or trying out ideas, that learning will really 'stick'.

**Myth 2.** *'Excellent lessons just 'happen''.*

**Reality** – Outstanding lessons are carefully planned and thoroughly prepared by the teacher. Not planning lessons well enough means that there is a danger of not addressing the students' needs and of the teacher talking too much or letting activities run on too long. All of these can undermine good learning.

# Some myths

**Myth 3.** *'Lesson plans must be rigidly followed'.*

**Reality** – Good lesson plans are important as they help you think about what you want to achieve and what resources you need to use to match your learners' needs. Without a good plan it is less likely that you will teach an effective lesson. But students are unpredictable; sometimes you realise that you have planned something that is too easy or too difficult. Slavishly following an unsuitable lesson plan is never a good idea. Great teachers get feedback from their class and have the confidence to adapt their lesson accordingly.

**Myth 4.** *'Outstanding lessons only happen with 'high ability' or perfectly behaved classes'.*

**Reality** – Provided you create suitable, appropriate challenge, pupils of *all* abilities can achieve in outstanding lessons. Likewise, we are in a position to manage pupil behaviour so that it does not detract from our lessons. (More hints on this later.)

# Some myths

 **Myth 5.** *'You can only tell if a lesson is excellent by the end of that lesson'.*

 **Reality** – In outstanding lessons teachers rarely leave reviewing the learning to the last five minutes of class. An excellent teacher periodically reviews how the lesson is going by checking how the pupils are responding and what they are learning.

**Myth 6.** *'Only a stern disciplinarian can teach an excellent lesson'.*

**Reality** – Good behaviour and order are essential – but pupils respond better to praise and reward, than iron control. If pupils are silent – how do you know they are learning?

**Myth 7.** *'You can only teach an excellent lesson after x number of years' teaching'.*

**Reality** – New teachers and experienced teachers teach excellent lessons. It is the impact of what you do on the pupils' learning that is most important – not the number of years' service.

# So what does make a great lesson?

Focusing on the reality of outstanding lessons helps us to see what is important. When you observe a fantastic lesson you see that many factors contribute towards its success.

In recent years, lessons judged to be outstanding have focused less on the teacher's demonstration of their expert knowledge and more on the **students** and **their learning** and **independence**. Excellent lessons these days aren't about the teacher showing off how much they know. The crucial questions are:

- What helps the pupils learn?
- How are they encouraged to be independent?
- How much progress have they made in the lesson?

# Four factors

In excellent lessons the four areas below are carefully balanced. Think about how they contribute towards quality learning in your own lessons. Have *you* got them nicely balanced?

1. **Teacher Subject Expertise**
   - Teacher knows their subject area
   - They create engaging and memorable strategies for passing this on
   - They are able to anticipate, respond and correct misconceptions

2. **Pupil Engagement**
   - Safe environment in which to learn and share ideas
   - Good management of classroom behaviour
   - Pupils are actively involved in the lesson and learn from each other

3. **Effective Climate for Learning**
   - Positive atmosphere – plenty of praise
   - Pupils feel able to respond and take a chance
   - Teacher fosters pupils' self-confidence

4. **Pupils Develop Independence in Their Learning**
   - Pupils know what 'good' work looks like and how to achieve it
   - They are aware of what their next learning steps are and how to tackle them
   - They are able to work independently and discuss their ideas

How would you know that these areas were being addressed if you observed a lesson?

# What pupils say

The best lessons have a positive impact on pupils and help them make a great deal of progress. Pupils' comments are often very insightful about what makes a great lesson:

'I have enjoyed it! And I actually know that I have learnt a lot.'

'Realising that I've achieved my best and getting this as feedback from the teacher.'

'The bell rings and the lesson has just flown by – bad lessons go on forever.'

'I have actually learnt how to do things for myself, not just been talked at.'

'Miss never accepts the first answer so I'm always being challenged in her lessons!'

'Realising I have got much better at essay writing and knowing how to improve my work.'

'Knowing that the teacher is with us and wanting us to do really well. Less than the best isn't good enough for him.'

# Pupil perspective counts!

Given that pupils are the main focus of the lesson, and that excellent lessons include pupil participation and active involvement, it makes sense to ask *your* pupils what they think of their lessons and to find out what makes an outstanding learning experience.

Ask for feedback on what works – and importantly *'What would make the lesson even better?'* There are many ways of doing this, but a simple and effective one is to give students a sticky note on which to record their thoughts as the lesson ends. Ask them to write on the top half:

- All of the things about the lesson that helped them learn
- What they feel they actually learnt from the lesson today

They should fill in as many ideas as they can.

Then, ask them to write in the bottom half: *What would have improved my learning today?*

- What helped me learn today?

- I learnt:

- My learning would have improved if:

# Listening to pupils improves learning

Understanding how your pupils see your lesson and what helps them learn is crucial for making improvements in your teaching.

CASE STUDY

*One GCSE Business Studies teacher asked for some feedback after teaching a revision lesson. Several pupils said they would have found the lesson more effective if it had tackled the aspects of the topic **they** actually struggled with – rather than the one **she** thought they found hard. They wanted to have been asked which areas of the topic they found most difficult and for revision to be related to this. Now she always makes sure she asks pupils how they feel about what they are learning.*

Regularly asking pupils to feed back – whether by sticky note, questionnaire or other means – will provide useful insights. If several pupils come up with the same idea for improvement, you might pursue this in your next lesson. If you need to try out different teaching strategies, you could ask a colleague to observe you to see if they can offer some ideas, or you could refer to it explicitly in the next lesson and ask students for suggestions about tackling it.

What do pupils think about your lessons? What can you celebrate? What could be made even better?

# Spreading the word

Involving pupils in feeding back on lessons is good practice, but does it need to be just about your own lessons? We all know that other teachers will be doing great things in their classrooms – behind closed doors. There isn't time to watch lots of other lessons, but finding out what other teachers' 'best bits' and 'top strategies' are can be very useful.

**CASE STUDY**

*One school took this idea of pupil review further. They set up a simple online pupil survey (try, **www.surveymonkey**) asking students about the best strategies different teachers employed to help them become better learners. The results provided detailed information about a wide range of lessons and the top strategies were shared with all staff. Internal training took place to ensure that the successful tactics and teaching ideas were adopted in a wider variety of classes and subjects. The result: improved teaching and learning!*

Hint: Giving pupils time to complete this survey in school, rather than as homework, led to a better and more detailed response.

# Dealing with negative feedback

Sometimes, unable to articulate their frustration or lack of motivation, pupils make unhelpful comments. (And, whatever you do, a tiny number of pupils will be dismissive, even after a cracking lesson.) But if you regularly get negative comments from a range of pupils, think about what they may be telling you – and what you might need to do about it:

| Typical Comments | Suggested Actions – Which would you do? In which order would you do them? What else could be considered? |
|---|---|
| 'It's boring….' | Check that the pupils know **why** they are doing something. |
| 'But we did this last lesson/week/year?' | Explain what you are looking for in successful work at this level. |
| | Make clear how *this* work is different from previous work. |
| 'I don't understand what to do….' | Ask them to explain their concerns in detail. |
| 'It's too easy/ too hard….' | Break up the task into sections and give plenty of praise. |
| | Investigate whether this is a widespread feeling in the class. |
| | Ask a friend to watch you with the class – do they note the same issues? |

Myth vs Reality

 Developing Great Relationships

 Planning Outstanding Lessons

 It's About Them – Not You!

 The X Factor

 Resources and Techniques

 Motivate 'em!

 Moving Forward

# Developing Great Relationships

# Step 1. Get to know your pupils

Teaching several hundred students and getting to know them individually at the start of the school year may seem like a huge effort. Teachers who really get to know their pupils are rewarded by increased pupil motivation. Importantly, they have the ability to detect and act immediately on any signs of underachievement. So take all opportunities to talk to students outside of lessons, and in those moments before lessons begin.

Learn their names quickly. Knowing students' names gives you power and credibility! To help you learn them, play name games such as going around the class saying: 'Ross likes rhubarb, Adam likes apples and Amy likes apricots... etc'

# Step 1. Get to know your pupils

**True story:**

I coached a teacher who was struggling with many of her classes. Despite teaching them for over three months, she didn't know many of their names. She'd given up:

'I'm just one of those people who find it too hard to learn names!'

She expected her students to tackle the challenge of learning French, but didn't persevere in learning their names. This contributed towards the pupils' declining behaviour and lack of effort – it appeared that she didn't really care about them, as she couldn't even refer to them by name.

# Step 2. Value pupils as individuals

How well do you know *your* pupils as individuals?

1. Pick a class and, taking a blank piece of paper, write down from memory all of your pupils' names. Most teachers find that the naughtiest, cleverest and best-behaved students spring to mind. Did you forget any? These 'missing few' are often the forgotten faces in the classroom. They might be quiet and well behaved, or silent and sullen. Either way, these 'forgotten' pupils sit on the margins of lessons and are often ignored. Take particular note of those names you forgot and make them the centre of your teaching for the next few lessons – then rotate the spotlight.

2. When giving feedback or sorting out activities, watch out for always starting with pupils whose names are at the very start or end of the alphabet. Begin sometimes in the middle.

3. Likewise, watch out for favouring some pupils with your attention more than others, particularly those that sit right at the front (under your nose!) or back of the classroom.

# Step 3. Share *your* attention and *their* good work

Clearly all of the above help to set the groundwork for great teacher/pupil relationships. However, excellent lessons are about ensuring pupils make **progress** in their learning. Excellent teachers really understand where a child is with their learning and adopt simple strategies to ensure that everybody gets a share of attention and help:

* If you want to see a child about a correction or aspect of their work, place coloured sticky notes on their exercise books to remind you when you come to hand them back. Pupils are notorious for avoiding the 'see me' comment, but having these conversations with individual pupils is vital for explaining misconceptions
* Use examples of students' work at the start of a lesson to highlight good practice and to explain improvements. Make sure you rotate this across the pupils and that you teach pupils how to comment constructively on each other's work. This gets everybody involved and helps highlight strengths and areas for development

# Step 4. Be informed

If pupils are to make exceptional progress, teachers need to know them as individuals. Do you know:

- Where exactly each pupil is in their current learning and understanding?

- What more should be expected of them? What are their previous targets, levels and test scores? What are they predicted to achieve? What have been their previous successes and failures?

- Any information about them that influences their ability to learn, eg Special Educational Needs information, disabilities, or aspects of their personal or family life that might affect their ability or confidence to learn

You need this information so that you can challenge your students and expect the best from them. Understanding them and their specific learning needs means you can help them to overcome any barriers to their learning.

Myth vs Reality

 Developing Great Relationships

 Planning Outstanding Lessons

 It's About Them – Not You!

 The X Factor

 Resources and Techniques

 Motivate 'em!

 Moving Forward

# Planning Outstanding Lessons

# From learning to doing

An outstanding lesson starts with a blank sheet of paper, but before you start planning lots of exciting activities for your pupils, first consider what it is you really want them to learn. There is a significant distinction between **learning** and **doing**.

Many lessons go awry because the teacher is too focused on the students completing a task or activity (doing), rather than on what they want the pupils to **learn**. The sequence for planning lessons should be:

1.  Knowing where your pupils are in their learning. (This might involve looking at information about individuals; data; previous learning, etc).

2.  Deciding what their next steps in learning are, ie the skill or knowledge you want them to develop in the lesson.

3.  Planning a range of engaging lesson activities to support this.

# Planning cycle for effective lessons

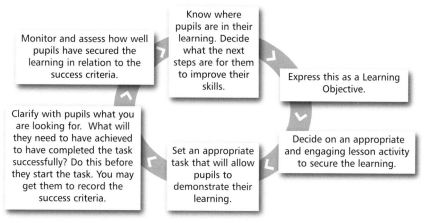

Know where pupils are in their learning. Decide what the next steps are for them to improve their skills.

Express this as a Learning Objective.

Decide on an appropriate and engaging lesson activity to secure the learning.

Set an appropriate task that will allow pupils to demonstrate their learning.

Clarify with pupils what you are looking for. What will they need to have achieved to have completed the task successfully? Do this before they start the task. You may get them to record the success criteria.

Monitor and assess how well pupils have secured the learning in relation to the success criteria.

- Notice how each stage follows on from and depends upon the previous stage
- Think about what might happen if any of the previous stages were omitted
- Think about the variety of ways to check and secure learning. Too much written work can demotivate pupils and exhaust teachers.

# When learning objectives help

It is often good practice to share lesson objectives with the class at the start of the lesson. In many classes these are recorded on the whiteboard and explained to the students. When used effectively they can:

- Signpost the learning, keying pupils in to the purpose of the lesson and making clear what the teacher will be focusing on
- Ensure that the lesson actually helps the pupils' learning because the activities clearly focus on the objective
- Make a distinction between the tasks and the learning. For example, the task might be to draw the classroom, but the objective to 'understand how to use shade and perspective'. The objective focuses the students on the actual skills they are acquiring
- Allow a clear way to review learning during and at the end of the lesson (by returning to the objectives and discussing how far they have been achieved)

# When learning objectives hinder

However, if *every* lesson starts with an explanation of what pupils will be learning – and especially if students have to copy this down – lessons soon become tedious, routine and ineffective. Those who are slow writers or who find literacy challenging will struggle. Sometimes you will want to:

- Surprise the pupils (starting lessons the same way every day precludes this)
- Make them think! (eg by putting some objects on the table to introduce a topic and getting the class to speculate, or by using a picture to stimulate creative thought)
- Disguise the 'unpopular topic' by getting them to succeed with an activity that it later transpires is related to this topic, eg solving a 'puzzle' which turns out to be an introduction to mathematical equations
- Develop pupil independence by getting them to consider: *What is it you already know about this topic? And what do you think you need to know about it?*

Outstanding teachers ensure it is clear what pupils are learning but they know there are many ways to convey this.

# Key ingredients

Great lessons have a range of ingredients, but it is not as simple as ensuring that every lesson has a carefully marshalled objective, success criteria and a plenary. Consider the following description of a lesson:

> *'All the students worked incredibly hard. They met the demanding challenges set by the teacher. Everybody was motivated and engaged. At the end of the lesson one pupil said: 'That was really good. I learnt loads, but it was fun too.'*
>
> *The teacher who had been observed said, 'But I didn't write the learning objectives on the board, and we ran out of time for a plenary because the students had so many questions about what they had been doing and we talked about them instead. It can't be an outstanding lesson can it?'*

Yes it can! All the pupils knew what they were learning. They knew what they had to do to become successful in that lesson and achieved it. They made excellent progress.

Outlining the discussed objectives is one way of starting lessons but it is by no means prescriptive. Likewise, the discussion at the end of the lesson enabled students to show their learning to a greater extent than the plenary the teacher had initially planned.

# Be flexible

Good lesson planning is crucial because it makes you think about what your class can do and where you want them to go next. But don't be a slave to your lesson plan. It is just a 'plan' and, like all plans, may need to be adapted.

Flexibility means that you adapt your lesson if it is not working, for example:

- You 'speed' up parts of a lesson if the class are finding them too easy
- If pupils have not understood it, you re-explain or explore their misconceptions
- You use a resource from current news/school events to explain your ideas
- You get students involved in explaining the main idea or demonstrating their skills
- You change tack completely owing to an unforeseen change in circumstances, eg failure of technology/response to the mood or attitude or your class. A new lively 'drama-based activity' might not be appropriate if the class has just arrived, angry about the events in the previous lesson

# Stay flexible

Staying flexible means that when you see a good learning opportunity you can seize it:

- Take the opportunity to allow pupils' questions and respond to their ideas
- Adapt your teaching strategies and timings to deepen pupils' knowledge and think about ideas, eg nobody responds to your questions, so you give the class five minutes to think up several ideas in pairs, or you show them work from another class to stimulate ideas
- Make links between other areas of the curriculum, eg they mention that they've been studying the slave trade in History and it is the theme of the poem you are studying, so you ask them about it and let them develop connections
- Respond to learning opportunities such as adding further challenge or sophistication to what you are doing, eg changing the task set or creating an additional challenge: *'I don't just want a linear story, include a flash back.'*
- Develop students' understanding and independence, eg by allowing thinking time, developing partner working and training them to self- and peer-mark

# Poor planning

While flexibility is important, it can signal poor planning if it is used it as an excuse not to prepare properly or think about your lessons carefully enough. Signs include:

- Having 'wasted' time at the end or start of a lesson where pupils have nothing clear to do

- Failing to prepare pupils adequately for exams because there are suddenly 'not enough lessons' left to cover the exam specification or scheme of work

- Pupils leaving lessons unclear about what it is they have been learning and how it fits in to the 'bigger picture' of what they are studying

- Pupils spending too long on tasks and getting distracted

- Allowing pupils to 'sidetrack' you for long discussions about topics not related to learning

It's easy to fall into some of these traps, but being aware of the pitfalls and having a good lesson plan helps us to avoid them, particularly when we know we have the confidence to change tack if things aren't working.

# The lesson within the sequence of work

An effective lesson does not take place in isolation. It should be part of a series of learning episodes. Effective teachers have the 'big picture' in mind. This might be the learning for the whole year or term. They then break this 'long-term' plan down, through objectives or skills, into medium-term plans.

Excellent teachers think about this series first, deciding on the overall outcomes they want for their students. They are clear about what they want pupils to gain from the sequence of lessons and what skills they need to master by the end of, say, four weeks. In this way they create a series of effective and connected individual lessons.

An outstanding lesson usually makes use of prior learning by:

* Encouraging pupils to make links between what they have previously studied
* Relating individual lessons to the whole picture and overall lesson objectives
* Encouraging pupils to reflect on how the learning is connected over a series of lessons
* Helping pupils to think about what their next steps in learning are

# Why sequences are important

If lesson planning starts with the overall picture of what pupils need to achieve and the skills they need to master over a particular period, it is more likely that individual lessons will:

- Form a coherent programme of study
- Make sense to the learner, as they understand the progression of skills and can see their own progress
- Cover all the skills, knowledge or competencies necessary for the programme of study
- Allow the learning to be staged to match the needs of the learner
- Show evidence of progression and mastery of skills
- Help the teacher plan well-focused lessons that show progression

# FAST starts

You have already thought about what you want your students to learn and you are clear about the lesson objectives. Remember to do things **FAST**!

 **Focus** – Get the pupils focused on the task in hand, settled and in the right frame of mind for learning.

 **Activity** – Get them going! Activities need to be simple, quick to set up, but sufficiently challenging to make them worthy of completion.

 **Systems** – Have well understood strategies for managing homework, forgotten pens, latecomers, etc.

 **Teach!** – Get on with the **learning** and don't waste time! Remember, getting them settled and quiet is a means to an end, not the end in itself.

# Developing effective systems

Many potentially excellent lessons are derailed by a lack of effective systems. Minor issues escalate into time-wasting and tempers fray. Before you know it 15 minutes (or more!) of the lesson have been wasted.

Your systems and 'hot spots' will be different according to what subject or age group you teach. However, you need to think about what can disrupt, and decide how you will tackle it so that the lesson and learning stay on track.

Don't let things like missing homework, not having pens, or other minor infringements derail your lesson. Set up systems for these that don't take your time and attention from the class, eg have a stock of pens for loan, but borrowers have to collect in the books at the end of the lesson; or record their names so you can track persistent offenders. Pick up homework or lateness issues once the class is well underway, rather than holding up the lesson in those crucial first few minutes.

- What are your 'hot spots' (issues than can derail your start)?
- How could you plan to manage these better or even prevent them altogether?

# Effective systems – one teacher's ideas

| Hot Spots | Short-term Action | Long-term Action | Review |
|---|---|---|---|
| Year 8 pupils fail to bring pens to class. | Give out pens labelled with my name to get lesson started quickly. | Raise with form tutor – suggest equipment checks.<br><br>Adopt rewards for those who regularly bring equipment.<br><br>Have a pen monitor. | Many more pupils are bringing pens 26/30 – still good idea to have some spares to loan.<br><br>Pupils like being a pen monitor and tell each other off if they don't bring pens! Pupils don't like this and more bring pens. |
| Some pupils fail to complete homework and argue at start of lesson. | | | |
| Pupils arrive late after lunch. | | | |

# Mystery and surprise

Routines can often be useful in settling behaviour and establishing teaching methods. They can reinforce clear expectations and steady a class so that they are ready to learn. Too much routine, however, can lead to boredom. Methods for starting and signalling the learning in the lesson need to be sufficiently interesting and engaging. This often means doing things differently and keying the pupils in to the learning, eg:

- Starting the lesson with a mystery. This might be a puzzle or a video clip or example of a mistake in a piece of work and asking pupils to solve it for you. This can be a way of stimulating students' curiosity and awakening their intellect

- Showing them interesting artefacts, getting them to pose questions or asking them to relate learning to their previous lesson will grab them in a way that referring them to the next page of their text book won't

Even if you do regularly ask pupils to complete a similar style of activity, liven it up by changing how you do it, eg using pair, individual and group tasks. Remember, variety creates interest and interest generates pupil engagement!

# Get them hooked!

## True story:

I was once asked to teach a lesson to a notoriously difficult class in a school in challenging circumstances. I was told, 'I doubt you'll be able to get them to write anything at all.'

Starting the lesson with a blank sheet of paper would have been a disaster. Instead, showing an example of work with some obvious and less obvious errors grabbed students' attention (they love spotting mistakes!) and allowed me an opportunity to praise them.

They went on to develop their own written work and showed some impressive progress.

# Get them hooked!

Expert teachers 'hook' pupils' interest as soon as they enter the room.

The following hooks work:

- Using a picture to provoke interest and stimulate debate. In Geography I saw pupils fascinated as a close-up picture was gradually revealed. They were challenged to speculate about what it was and how it related to the new topic of climate change
- Starting with a challenge connected to the topic, eg providing an extract of text and getting students to find five clues about it, or showing a partial chart or diagram and getting them to predict how it will be completed
- Asking pupils to think of five questions that they want to solve in the lesson

# Activities that engage

Get those first few minutes right and you will set the tone for a successful lesson. As we have seen, an engaging activity, (but one that is simple to set up), is a great way to start a lesson. Try adding a dash of competition and all pupils will be desperate to impress. Think about setting such 'challenges' in pairs for maximum pupil participation.

However, don't get entertainment muddled with effective learning. Good learning can be fun, but the activity needs to be more than just entertaining; it has to be challenging and has to help the pupils learn. When planning an opening activity, ask yourself:

- Is it time specific?
- Is it clear what pupils have to do?
- Is it suitably challenging for all class members?
- Is it a good way of introducing or provoking interest in the next stage of learning? (Or does it help revise key ideas from the previous lesson?)

# The acid test for starters

How effective do you think the following Y9 English starters are?:

**Starter 1** *'You have two minutes. Write down all the words you can think of that begin with P.'*

**Starter 2** *'You have two minutes. How many words can you think of that mean 'pain'? Then, take two minutes using a thesaurus/ dictionary to check meanings and refine your ideas.'*

In task 1 pupils might be initially engaged, but it is so wide and offers such little challenge, that they will soon lose heart. How will such a wide task be developed into a good lesson?

In task 2 pupils are given a reasonably high level of challenge. Dictionaries and thesauruses enable them to develop independence and check definitions. In the lesson I watched, students went on to write their words on sticky notes and placed them on a continuum line across the board, justifying their placement. Were their words mild in meaning (eg *'twinge'*) or did they express intense pain (eg *'agony'*)? This made a superb introduction to the reading of a war poem and led to a high level discussion of shades of meaning implied by different words: excellent!

# Sparkling starters

Have a go at the following tried and tested starters:

- Give out three terms or items from last lesson and ask pupils to pick the odd one out and give reasons why

- Think of five! Students must list or recall five features or things that connect to the topic

- Remind pupils of the topic from last lesson by asking them to come up with six key words. In pairs each person needs to talk about the topic for two minutes trying to recall all key information

- Ask some pupils from the previous lesson to devise a starter for the whole class. (This can be a good and interesting way of providing stretch and challenge for more able pupils)

- Give out cards with a number of different ideas on. Get the class to either rank order the best ideas (and be prepared to defend their choices), or structure the ideas in the correct order. The fact that they have to move the cards will promote discussion

# Finding new ways to start lessons

Good lessons engage pupils straight away and make them feel that purposeful learning is taking place. There can be a limit to the number of ideas you can come up with for engaging lesson openings. Why not observe a fellow teacher and ask yourself:

- How do they start the lesson in an effective way? How do they grab the pupils' attention right from the start?
- What strategies and systems are in place to signal to the pupils that the lesson has started and that quality learning is expected?
- What engaging and appropriate teaching strategies are used to absorb and focus the pupils in those all important first few minutes of the lesson?
- Does the teacher involve pupils in setting out the start of the lesson? 'Power Teaching' film clips on YouTube show some engaging examples of American pupils feeding back on each other's work in a way that promotes both pupil independence and confidence

# Do and review

It is vital that by the end of a lesson pupils are clear about what they have learnt. Establish this by getting them to review and reflect on how effectively they think they have met the objectives. Or even more simply by asking, *'What have we learnt today?'* and *'What can we now do?'* or *'What are we better at doing than we were yesterday?'*

It is important to get our students to tell us what they feel they have learnt as it's not always what we hoped we had taught them!

Some pupils may well be too young to review and reflect upon their learning by themselves but skilful questioning of even the youngest children can help them think about what new skills they have mastered. In some cases, it will be your observations of a student and their work that will tell you whether or not the objective has been met.

To sum up:
- Plan lessons by focusing on what pupils are expected to learn
- Plan activities that support this
- Review the learning with your pupils and plan for their next steps

Myth vs
Reality

 Developing
Great
Relationships

 Planning
Outstanding
Lessons

 It's About
Them – Not
You!

 The X Factor

 Resources
and
Techniques

 Motivate
'em!

 Moving
Forward

# It's About Them – Not You!

# Pupils are centre stage in great lessons

A silent lesson is rarely an outstanding lesson. In outstanding lessons pupils are **active in their own learning** and **engaged**.

The real test of a great lesson is what the pupils can do as a result of it. In the very best lessons, pupils learn a great deal; they absorb new skills and information and are able to do something for themselves – not just in that day's lesson, but days, weeks or months later they can still recall it and put it into practice! Their progress is demonstrable.

However, getting pupils to become independent learners can be a real challenge. Obstacles can include: apathy, lack of confidence, and an over-reliance on the teacher or teaching assistant completing the work for them.

This chapter is about **fostering independence**. The following pages offer six steps towards that goal.

The diagram below shows how **pupil progress** is related to **pupil independence**. It highlights the importance of clear guidance and high expectations from the teacher and how pupils need to be taught to become independent and self-reflective.

Pupils make exceptional progress and enjoy lessons

Increased pupil motivation and independence

Pupils able to reflect upon their learning and their next steps in learning

Teacher expertise identifies next learning steps and shares them with pupils

Teacher use engaging and appropriate teaching strategies to challenge all pupils

Teacher plans lesson that makes learning objective clear to pupils and addresses all needs

Teacher has good knowledge of pupils, their previous learning and what can be expected of them

# STEP 2 Defining the challenge

Many pupils would rather you told them the answers or found solutions for them! Even some 17-year-old students have been known to say, *'Just tell me the answer,'* when asked to think about, work out, investigate or research something.

Similarly, in Early Years, doing something for young children, rather than letting them learn through exploration, can be a temptation.

In both cases, providing the resources for pupils to find things out for themselves is the best way to help them learn.

It might take two minutes to give somebody the correct answer and it might take 20 minutes for them to find out the solution for themselves, but which is likely to help them remember how to do it again and lead to long-term retention of knowledge or skills?

'Tell me and I'll forget; show me, I may remember; involve me and I'll understand.'
**(Chinese Proverb)**

# **STEP 3** Developing active and engaged learners

Consider the following questions about your lessons this week:

- How much do you talk? How much do your students talk? Is the balance right?
- We soon 'zone out' and stop listening if somebody talks for too long, or if an activity overruns. How do you avoid this happening?
- If we are not made to stop, think and reflect on our learning we may just 'go through the motions' in a lesson. *How* do you make them think? How *hard* do you make them think?
- Breaking lessons into chunks of activities and periodically reviewing learning helps pupils to retain and make sense of what they have learnt. How long are your 'learning chunks'? Do they engage and sustain pupils' interest?
- Predictable activities and arrangements can make some lessons boring and, in turn, lead to disruption. How much variety is there in your lessons?
- Do you sometimes set 'unexpected' challenges to keep students alert and interested?

 # STEP 4 Lesson strategies

Outstanding teachers suggest these simple strategies for improving pupil independence. Which ones do you already use? Which ones might be worth trying?

- **Start lessons with a statement**. Pupils agree, disagree and prove or disprove it. They must be able to justify their answers!

- **'Just a minute'**. In pairs students time each other talking about a topic for a minute, making sure they cover the most important aspects

- **Present it**. Pupils investigate different aspects of a topic and present their findings to the class in whichever way they think is most helpful, eg: power point, poster, role play, wall display, quiz, podcast. The important factor is whether the message is received by the class in a way that makes it memorable

- **New partners**. Create different seating plans and paired work partners, so that pupils are used to working with a wide range of individuals. This reduces dependency and resistance to working with new people

- **Assess yourself**. Give students a list of strategies and ground rules for working with partners and peer reviewing. They assess how effectively they have worked together

# STEP 4 Lesson strategies

- **Resources**. Make available a good range of resources such as dictionaries, thesaurus, reference books and the internet so that pupils can look up things for themselves

- **Display**. Use displays to promote active involvement by eg: posing questions, showing annotated versions of pupils' work, highlighting key vocabulary. Pupils can refer to them and use them to improve or check their work

- **Teacher – last resort!** Jim Smith in *The Lazy Teacher's Handbook* refers to '3 before me!' He expects students to think of three ways of finding out the answers before resorting to asking the teacher for assistance. Try it!

# STEP 5 How other staff can help

Teaching an outstanding lesson isn't always just about us and our interactions with our pupils. If we have other adults in the lessons they need to have a positive impact on learning too and, as the teacher, part of our role is to ensure that they offer 'precise, targeted support'. In excellent lessons *all* staff:

- Are clear about their role in the lesson. They know what is expected of them
- Understand the tasks set and know not only what pupils should be doing, but also the success criteria for a piece of work. They can then help students focus on the important aspects of the task rather than the incidentals
- Know any SEN /other information about pupils so they can work with them effectively
- Assist and motivate pupils, but **do not** create a dependency. They are encouraging and sensitive but expect pupils to learn and think independently. They question and guide students rather than giving them the answers or 'helping' too much

# **STEP 5** How other staff can help

Building good relationships with our teaching assistants is important. They should feel comfortable about discussing things that have gone well, asking for further explanation, and suggesting improvements. Feedback is a two-way process and we need to promote dialogue among the adults in the room.

Great teaching assistants really help us to improve learning in our lessons by:

- Feeding back successes, failures and next steps. Hearing honest feedback about how our strategies have supported or hindered a students' progress helps us appreciate what has worked so that the next steps in learning can be secured

- Ensuring that it is clear whether a student has had specific help with completing aspects of their work

- Giving students clear and precise feedback on their work that relates to their next steps in learning and helps them make really good progress

# STEP 6 Spotting signs of independence

The following are signs that a teacher has fostered successful independent learning.

Pupils:

1. Engage in debates and discussions.
2. Ask questions of themselves and the teacher.
3. Think and speculate about the lesson's link with prior learning.
4. Are able to make links with other subjects.
5. Happily work independently, in pairs and in a variety of group situations.
6. Are resourceful – they know how to find out things for themselves and make good use of resources before asking the teacher for help.
7. Enjoy and relish a challenge! They aren't afraid to try things out.
8. Are not fazed by getting it wrong. They know that this is an important part of the learning process.
9. Review and reflect upon their learning, sometimes in the lesson plenary, through questions, evaluations or through regular learning logs.
10. Can articulate what their next goal or target is and what they need to do to get there.

Myth vs
Reality

 Developing
Great
Relationships

 Planning
Outstanding
Lessons

 It's About
Them – Not
You!

 The X Factor

 Resources
and
Techniques

 Motivate
'em!

 Moving
Forward

# The X factor

# Harnessing the X factor

What is it that turns an okay lesson into a great one? What gives it the extra pizzazz, helping pupils to enjoy what they are learning and to make impressive progress?

To help students achieve, you need to make them **believe in themselves**! This is absolutely essential for good learning. We all know that just telling somebody they are 'wonderful' or they can do something if they put their minds to it doesn't work – in fact, it can lead to great disappointment if they aren't supported to develop the tools for success. This is where **meaningful praise** comes in.

This chapter is about harnessing the 'X factor', ie **using praise** along with **aspects of Assessment for Learning** to boost self-esteem and equip pupils to learn. It's about empowering students so they can help *themselves* lead improvements.

We'll look first at praise (pages 59–61) then move on to peer- and self-assessment (pages 63 and 64), marking and feedback (page 65), target setting (pages 66–68), and, finally, effective questioning (pages 69–74).

# Praise and purpose

## Tips for making praise more effective:

Use **pupils' names** when you feed back to them. Students say they like this because it makes the comment more personal.

**Intelligence isn't fixed**. We want pupils to know that they *can* raise their achievement level if they take advice and apply themselves. We'll notice and reward their application.

Ensure you **praise effort and improvement** as well as (if not more than) attainment. Some children always come top in tests. Also reward those who try their best and who make rapid improvements.

**Be genuine!** Children see through 'false flattery'. If everything you see is '*wonderful*' or '*super*' the effect of such glib comments will soon wear off.

**Be specific** with your praise. It needs to be clear what you have liked and why, so students understand and can reflect on your comment.

**Proper Praise** = **Motivated Learners** = **Outstanding Lessons**

# ROIL your praise

High levels of meaningful praise encourage and reward pupils. However we can still give pupils areas to develop. **ROIL** your praise:

**R**   **R**oles and **R**esponsibilities. Allocating roles to pupils, eg 'stationery tsar' or book monitor gives them opportunities to shine and you the chance to praise. Rotate responsibilities so that *all* pupils receive praise. This is particularly important in changing behaviour patterns with difficult classes where finding something to praise can at times be hard. This is a start.

**O**   **O**pportunities. Ensure plenty of opportunities to thank pupils for their contributions. This is one of the quickest ways of setting up a great classroom climate.

**I**   **I**mprove. Be positive and suggest improvements. Phrase your comments carefully: *'Next time it would be even better if...'* You're giving constructive advice and keeping students' self esteem high!

**L**   **L**et others know! Think about 'praising up' – invite senior teachers to look at your pupils' work and use whole-school opportunities to display their achievements, eg in assemblies. You'll create a climate of achievement for these students *and* inspire others.

# Parents like hearing praise too

Students need to feel encouraged and motivated to give of their best. Their self-esteem needs to be high if they are to learn effectively in lessons. When self-esteem is high, people feel good about themselves – they believe they can do it!

Make regular efforts to contact parents and make good links with home. You can do this by sending a 'praise postcard', using stickers, or writing something positive in a pupil's planner. Phone their parents to say 'well done' about a particular project. The renewed effort from students in class when you do this will be worth it!

Involving parents
leads to **motivated pupils**
and **improved
relationships**

# Assessment for Learning matters

Assessment for Learning, or AfL, is about teacher *and* pupils using feedback to promote good progress. Some AfL happens within the lesson to check learning and help students make progress, eg:

- Questioning by the teacher, and by pupils
- Feedback – both verbal and written

Some of the techniques enable pupils to reflect and improve:

- Self-assessing their work
- Peer-assessing the work of a partner

Ultimately these lead students to setting and reviewing their own personal targets. Setting their own targets is not easy for pupils, but when done correctly it can really empower them. Research by Dylan Wiliam and Paul Black indicates that effective AfL leads to increased achievement and better motivated pupils. Ofsted frequently links aspects of AfL to outstanding teaching and learning.

# Peer- and self-assessment

If pupils know how to assess their own work and what to do to make it better, they will improve their learning. It is a win for both student and teacher.

It sounds simple – but it's actually a complex skill. Self- and/or peer-assessment can go wrong. It needs to be carefully set up and involves:

- Sharing and teaching the assessment criteria
- Showing examples
- Marking together as a class
- Setting up appropriate 'buddies'
- Reflection and target setting skills

If we demonstrate these processes with our classes, we can better help them understand how to succeed themselves. But it won't just magically happen; it takes time and practice.

# Peer- and self-assessment

Pupils need to be trained in how to assess work. It's helpful to follow a series of six steps:

| Step 1 | Step 2 | Step 3 | Step 4 | Step 5 | Step 6 |
|--------|--------|--------|--------|--------|--------|
| Be explicit about what is expected in a piece of work and share the success criteria with the class. | Show pupils anonymous exemplars of work, and model how to respond to them. | Get pupils as a group to comment and feedback on an anonymous piece of work. | Share and establish guidelines with the class on how to comment on each other's work. | When you feel sure that pupils are reflective and considerate of each other's work, involve them in feeding back on their own and their partner's work. | Pupils can then think about what their 'next steps in learning', their targets, should be. |

Excellent teachers know that they need to check students' marking of their work both to ensure it is effective and to gain feedback for their next lessons.

# Effective marking and feedback

Excellent lessons depend upon the teacher feeding back successes and areas for improvement to the pupil. Marking work and giving feedback helps you evaluate the effectiveness of your lesson. It identifies gaps in individual or groups of students' understanding.

Good feedback has five characteristics:

1. It is timely. Pupils lose interest (and the feedback loses impact) if they have to wait too long for it.

2. It is positive in nature. We all respond better to the carrot than the stick!

3. It is precise rather than vague: *'Good use of new vocab.'* (MFL), rather than *'Nice work.'*

4. It clearly indicates where improvements need to be made – again these are specific.

5. It frequently involves the pupil in responding or acting on the advice. This might involve improving the work, tracking the target, as on page 68, or verbally discussing it with the teacher.

# Helping pupils take ownership of their targets

In outstanding lessons students make excellent progress **and** they take ownership of this. To do so they need a simple way of recording and reflecting on their current standard of work and of tracking their targets for improvement.

It is imperative that individuals know where they are with their work so that they can go on to improve. For them to do so successfully, the following things need to be in place:

- Regular, quality feedback from the teacher that includes praise and that identifies clear strengths and targets for improvement
- Help in understanding their strengths and where they should be heading, so that it is clear what **they** need to do to improve on **their** work
- Lesson time set aside to allow pupils the opportunity to reflect on and improve their work (Many students won't automatically do this without guidance and allocated lesson time.)

# How am I doing?

There are certain things you can make sure your students know that will help them make really good progress. For example, pupils of all ages can be taught to:

- Talk about what they have been learning in lessons
- Know what they are working towards in terms of a grade or level (where appropriate)
- Know specifically what they need to do (what skills they need to master) to achieve it. This might involve you looking at the examination criteria with them, or showing them examples of these written in 'pupil speak'
- Have a simple recording mechanism (like the one on the next page) so that they can talk about their learning: where they are now, and what more they need to do next. It needs to be clear and easy to use. The idea is for the class teacher and pupil to work **together** to establish what the pupil needs to do to improve and to ensure that their work shows progress over time

# Ways of encouraging pupil ownership

I saw a superb mixed ability lesson where all students made outstanding progress. One simple system that the teacher employed – a chart – helped keep pupils focused on their individual steps for improvement.

**Pupils** had to note their target (usually from their marked work) and, most importantly, show evidence of where it had been met. This following up and recording of evidence meant that improvements actually took place and pupils did not become 'stuck' with the same target for weeks – or even months – and thereby fail to make progress.

| Date | Target | Where has it been met? Highlight where you have done this in your book using orange highlighter | Target signed off |
|------|--------|-----------------------------------------------|-------------------|
| 20/03/2011 | Use more interesting vocabulary | Pg 12, pg 13, pg 16 | Mrs K Jones |
| 01/04/2011 | Use and understand at least three rhetorical devices in non-fiction writing | Essay on uniform | |

# Questioning for challenge

Good quality questioning by the teacher is essential for ensuring good levels of challenge. Skilful questioning can transform an average lesson into an outstanding one. It is how a teacher checks pupils' progress. Unlike peer- and self-assessment, questioning is something that we do in **every** lesson!

Recent research by John Hattie* suggests some worrying aspects with many teacher questions. Some surveys, for example, found, **only** 20% of questions requiring thought by the students, 60% requiring factual recall and 20% procedural'.

If Hattie's research is common to many classrooms – and from my own observations I would suggest it is – it means that we often ask pupils undemanding questions. We need to ask questions that demand a higher level of thought.

*\* Visible Learning, by John Hattie. Routledge, 2009*

# Blooming questions!

One teacher who recognised weaknesses in his questioning technique devised a simple way to help him ask more challenging questions.

On his classroom wall he displayed various question openings, based loosely on 'Bloom's taxonomy', which identifies the different levels of challenge and demand in different types of questions.

Walking around the room, he used it to help him phrase his questions. It ensured that he always asked some higher level questions in his lessons, increasing the challenge for his students and improving his practice!

# Blooming questions!

| Knowledge questions | Comprehension questions | Applying the knowledge questions | Exploring/ analysing | Evaluating (Compare/ evaluate/ justify/ devise) |
|---|---|---|---|---|
| What did? | Why did? | How can you use..? | What if...? | What would you suggest to x? |
| When did? | What are the main aspects? | How would you change? | Consider...? | How could x be better in your work as a result of...? |
| Who did? | What does this mean? | Can you apply x to x? | Think about...? | How could you defend...? |
| Which word means? | Why has x been used? | Using this information how could you x? | Why does x appear best? | Think about... |
| | Can you explain briefly x? | | What issues are there with x? | Find three and explain why one is your best. |
| | | | Discuss... | |
| | | | Consider the reasons... | |

# Improving questioning technique

Weak questioning technique will prevent a lesson from being outstanding. Common problems include:

- **Not allowing enough thinking time**. Students need time to consider their answers

- **Expecting a particular answer** and not accepting or discussing divergent answers (When I say: *'Mmmm, yes...anyone else?'* I know it means I have stopped listening; I am just waiting for what I think is the right answer. It's a hard habit to break)

- **Not explaining or making use of wrong answers to improve learning**. Even if there is only one correct answer, asking pupils why they gave a different one is a way of understanding and correcting misconceptions. Great teachers see the lesson through their students' eyes, and that means understanding the reasons for their mistakes

- **Only asking certain people to participate**. Aim for 100% participation rate

- **Not asking challenging questions/ not differentiating questions**. Make 'em think!

# Honing your technique

Great questioning means that *all* pupils are involved and engaged. It can be very difficult to get all students to participate, but teachers who teach outstanding lessons have ideas for achieving this. Questions are differentiated so that they challenge all pupils appropriately. Ways of enhancing pupil involvement also include:

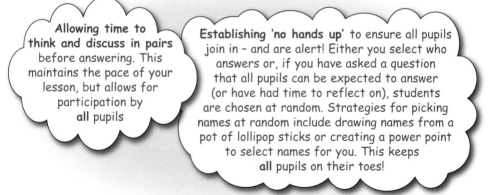

**Allowing time to think and discuss in pairs** before answering. This maintains the pace of your lesson, but allows for participation by **all** pupils

**Establishing 'no hands up'** to ensure all pupils join in – and are alert! Either you select who answers or, if you have asked a question that all pupils can be expected to answer (or have had time to reflect on), students are chosen at random. Strategies for picking names at random include drawing names from a pot of lollipop sticks or creating a power point to select names for you. This keeps **all** pupils on their toes!

# Honing your technique

**Targeting individuals** is important to ensure that questions engage and challenge everyone. A key rule is to ask the question first; say their name second! If pupils hear a specific child's name, they know they won't be asked and 'switch off'. They know it's not aimed at them, so why should they think!

**Following up.** Effective questioning challenges students and makes them think. Try to extend their learning by including follow up questions: 'Who else can add to this?' 'Who can refine that idea?' Effective questioning allows you to see how much your students are learning and lets you re-explain points or move the lesson on more quickly.

In excellent lessons pupils pose questions themselves. They think, reflect and build upon each other's answers. The teacher becomes a facilitator, rather than a director. Questioning becomes a means of exploration.

Myth vs Reality

 Developing Great Relationships

 Planning Outstanding Lessons

 It's About Them – Not You!

 The X Factor

 Resources and Techniques

 Motivate 'em!

 Moving Forward

# Resources and Techniques

# Effective use of resources

Choosing the right resources can make or break a lesson. When planning to use a particular resource or piece of equipment, ask yourself:

*   Is this the best way of helping pupils' learn?
*   Will all students be able to engage and interact with the learning?
*   Have I got all of the equipment and skills necessary to use it?
*   Do I use a range of different resources to promote a varied repertoire of teaching strategies in my lessons?

## True story:

I was observing a GCSE Maths lesson – the lesson plan looked great; it was an active investigation involving students measuring the length of their arms with a tape measure. There were only three tape measures for the whole class! Everything slowed down and pupils got distracted waiting their turn... ... you can guess the rest!

# ICT and outstanding lessons

ICT can be a very useful classroom tool. When used appropriately it can really promote pupil engagement and independence. However, unless you are an ICT teacher, it is just a tool. Use it as such, ie when it's the best way of helping pupils learn or of sharing ideas and resources – not just because it is there!

Effective teachers use ICT to add to the learning in a lesson. Websites, wikis and wall pages are ways of getting pupils to access learning in imaginative and interactive ways. They can also be used to reinforce or further the learning at home.

Check all websites and ICT tools to ensure that they are safe and appropriate for pupils – websites often change, so you need to check any web details you give, to ensure they are as expected.

# Effective ICT tools in lessons

Effective use of ICT might include:

- Using video clips and extracts from the internet as a way of stimulating interest:

  *A teacher helped students understand the emotion behind the issue of care homes by showing a five minute 'You Tube' clip where a man discussed placing his elderly mother in a 'home'. Using a clip showing real people's dilemmas helped pupils to discuss this sensitively.*

- Recording or videoing pupils' work. Visualisers (a piece of equipment rather like an advanced overhead projector) are great at capturing examples of pupils' work/ pictures. They highlight aspects of good work, and help discussion

  *A primary teacher dissected a flower on a visualiser allowing all the pupils to see in detail what was happening.*

- Making podcasts and placing useful resources on the school's virtual learning environment for students to access at home and for revision purposes

# Top ICT tools for teachers

There is an ever-growing range of ICT tools that can make a real contribution to a lesson's success. Some of these are ideal for sharing resources with other teachers or, where appropriate, with students.

**Google docs** is an innovative system that allows online collaboration and annotation of documents by multiple users. This can be used to set up interesting and engaging homework for older pupils. For a detailed guide sheet of how to set this up and use it, see www.bentley-davies.co.uk and follow the link under 'resources' for google docs.

**Wallwisher** is a simple application which allows a teacher to build an online notice-board and pose a question or idea. The website link is then passed to pupils or other staff so that they can access the page and post their own responses. These are displayed in the form of sticky notes and teachers can edit and check these before they are displayed. See www.wallwisher.com for more information.

# Using Wallwisher for homework

A teacher set up the following 'wall' (see next page) and gave year 7 pupils the web address so that they could post their homework. No email accounts are needed, so it is easy and safe to use.

Their homework was to write an engaging opening for a horror story, and the challenge: they had only one sentence with which to hook the reader.

It's a suitable activity for Wallwisher as it requires an open response; there isn't one expected answer. This is important as pupils will be able to see each other's posts before they write their own. The teacher set the privacy setting so that she had to read and agree each idea before they were publicly displayed. This is wise to stop inappropriate posts.

# Using Wallwisher for homework

Rain thrashed down; the house was totally cut off from its neighbours…
David

Ben knew from the moment he woke up that he was a dead man.
Ben

Old, crumbling and yellow with age, the ancient map showed a pathway to untold riches and almost certain death.
Alex

It should have been a great day, but it was turning out to be the day from hell!
Lucy

The house looked abandoned from the road: the hedges were high, ivy covered the front railings and cobwebs hung down by the door.
Sam

It was a dark and stormy night, 'just right for a murder', Joe thought
Ross

# Effective use of ICT by students

There are numerous ways students can benefit from using ICT in class and beyond, eg:

- Making podcasts, power points and web pages, etc
- Drafting work on screen, instead of 'copying up'. Encouraging pupils to think, craft, draft and redraft on screen helps them review and think more carefully about their writing. It's also incredibly motivating as they can improve the presentation of their work as well as easily change and develop content
- Researching key topics on the internet. Pupils need to be taught how to do this, including how to be selective and thoughtful about what they read and its provenance. Effective research isn't downloading hundreds of pages of information! Asking pupils to find the answer to specific questions, design a quiz, summarise the information they have read in just 25 words, display it in a different format, eg a diagram or fact sheet are all ways of ensuring that they are actually *reading* and, most importantly, *thinking about* what they have read

# Expand your repertoire

Using a range and variety of teaching strategies is crucial in teaching excellent lessons. Individuals like, respond to and enjoy learning in different ways. Some love to be dramatic and active; others like learning by reading or listening to the teacher or each other. You can often add to your repertoire by watching teachers teaching different subjects or year groups.

**CASE STUDY**

*In an 'A' Level PE lesson students were being taught memorable ways of revising the names and locations of bones in the foot. The teacher had a large diagram and students were in groups of four. Each person in the class had five minutes to look at the diagram before returning to their groups, where they pooled what they could remember to help them recreate the diagram. This involved strategy and teamwork, each member trying to remember different elements. The Geography teacher observing the lesson recognised the potential of this technique for teaching younger pupils about volcanoes.*

# Top teaching techniques

Great lessons are made from memorable learning experiences. Some of the following could help your pupils secure their learning. Great teachers:

**1** **Demonstrate the skills themselves** (it is even better if it doesn't work very well!). Pupils love critiquing a teacher's effort. Commenting on what was effective, or less effective is a good way of helping them learn.

**2** **Set puzzles**. Thinking challenges, for example, are a good way of getting pupils hooked in to the learning. Often a question, video clip, picture or teaser on the board (related to the topic) engages and interests the pupil in the topic.

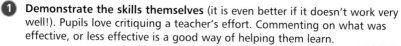

**3** **Review learning throughout the lesson** and don't just leave it to the end. (See page 94 for ideas for mini plenaries.)

**4** **Set activities as group challenges or quizzes** – good for engaging unmotivated pupils.

# Top teaching techniques

**5** **Use 'speed dating'** to help pupils prepare for exams. Students ask a question or share a piece of information with another person, then move on after three minutes. It is a rapid and fun way to check and review. It can be used with exam questions or for sharing a short piece of work such as an introduction to an essay.

**6** **Use circuit training** – setting up various 'stations' around the room with different tasks at each. Pupils work in pairs to complete these under pressure of time. A much more fun and interesting way to conduct exam revision than just going through past papers.

**7** **Encourage presentations**. Students really learn deeply if they are required to give a talk, presentation or demonstration of something. These are often best as short, focused activities. Asking pupils to write a page for a revision guide conveying key information for their peers is also a good way of consolidating knowledge.

# Giving instructions

With the right resources and a good repertoire of teaching techniques, you are well-equipped for teaching brilliant lessons. You might also need to hone your techniques for giving instructions and explanations. When you give good instructions:

- Everybody understands what they should be doing
- The time allocated for a task is clear and sets a good pace to the lesson
- Pupils have the opportunity to ask and clarify instructions before the activity is underway

Lessons can go wrong if instructions are not clear. The main errors teachers make when issuing instructions are:

- Giving them out in a noisy environment
- Not being specific enough about what we want pupils to do
- Not clarifying the success criteria for a piece of work. (Good practice involves giving out a self-check list, or showing an exemplar of work first.)
- Not checking students' understanding of a task before they start
- Allowing too long to complete a task – instead try breaking it down, stopping periodically and reviewing

# Tips for improving instructions

When you give instructions in your lessons, think about the **START!**

 **Silence** – insist on it! Effective teachers have a range of strategies for this, such as signalling for quiet with a raised hand or other gesture. This catches pupils' attention and gets them focused and ready to listen.

**Time frames** – issue clear time frames for the work to be completed and signal this throughout the lesson, eg *'You have five minutes left...two minutes to decide on your final answer...'* This helps keep the pace of the lesson purposeful.

**Ask** – ask a student to recap the instructions verbally. This helps ensure that everybody has understood what is being asked of them.

**Rephrase** – rephrase your instructions if you feel pupils have misunderstood or are unsure.

**Two ways or more** – where possible, reinforce verbal instructions with a written reminder on a worksheet, whiteboard or display so that pupils and TAs can double check stages of work.

# Explaining it differently

It is not uncommon for students to misunderstand or become confused by a main idea or concept. This can be distressing for the teacher, especially if we feel that we have already explained it clearly. If pupils don't understand a concept, try some of the following:

* Asking another student to explain the idea
* Asking the pupil to articulate what it is about the concept that they don't understand
* Using a comparison or analogy
* Using a diagram, picture, chart – something visual – to support your verbal or written explanation
* Asking other staff members what techniques they use to teach this area
* Research different ways of tackling this topic via the internet or your subject association

And remember, to be successful most of us need to see **good examples** of something before we tackle it – whether this is watching a clip of a dance movement, seeing a demonstration of how to use a piece of equipment or examining a section of a good essay.

Myth vs
Reality

 Developing
Great
Relationships

 Planning
Outstanding
Lessons

 It's About
Them – Not
You!

 The X Factor

 Resources
and
Techniques

 Motivate
'em!

 Moving
Forward

# Motivate 'em!

# Talk for motivation

One of the most important things we can do to ensure a successful lesson is to think about our own communication.

How we speak to students is crucial in getting them 'onside' and in helping to motivate them about their learning. Excellent teachers think carefully about how they phrase things. They express their interest in the topic and in their students through their voice and word choice. They use pupils' names and inject warmth and humour into their interactions.

They convey their passion for their subject and, despite tiredness, life's annoyances and pupils' reactions, they stay calm. It can be very difficult to maintain a professional front when a child is being deliberately rude or provocative. However we need to stay calm to engage our pupils and must try to avoid showing frustration when pupils say they 'don't understand' yet again, or engage in low-level poor behaviour.

These skills (and they can be hard to maintain at all times) make the difference between pupils giving a task their best shot and simply giving up.

# Change your comments, change your class!

Good teachers know that simple changes in the way they communicate can make the difference between pupils co-operating and causing disruption:

| Negative comment and subtext | Motivating comment and subtext |
|---|---|
| *You will find this topic really hard 8P.* **You are going to struggle; you won't enjoy it and probably can't do it.** | *You are ready for the next big challenge 8P* **It will be difficult, but fun: I believe in you!** |
| *Start work!* **It's hard labour time!** | *Right class let's get on! Off you go.* **Let's get going...it will be fine. We need to get cracking...** |
| *Right, time for a test! If you don't get a good enough mark you will have to re-take it.* **It will be hard; you will more than likely fail. I reign by inflicting fear.** | *Here's a quiz/challenge. There'll be merits for people who improve on last week's score.* **It's going to be fun but a challenge, with rewards for those who put in the effort.** |
| *Absolutely no talking!* **It is my regime! Lessons aren't meant to be engaging or fun.** | *We're going to have 15 minutes quiet time while we get on.* **I would like you to focus for a specific time but I know that absolute silence is not always desirable or realistic.** |

# Motivate through involvement

We only retain a small percentage of what we hear. In many 'just average' lessons the teacher talks too much and loses the class's attention. Learning slows down, and off-task behaviour starts to kick in. To keep students' attention and to make the learning memorable, keep things active and varied. Get students involved in their learning by:

- Keeping tasks focused, time-limited and active. Don't get them to do the same thing for too long. Break it up with discussions and group work

- Asking them to speculate, pose questions and debate. Adding an element of challenge involves students

- Getting them involved in the design of the lesson. Ask them what helps them really understand a topic and use this in your lesson

- Wherever possible, giving different pupils different roles or aspects of a topic to look at when working in groups. This added level of personal responsibility helps keep them motivated and interested. Even if you are just asking them to answer a range of questions, getting them to report back on a particular one helps them focus

# Reviewing learning during the lesson

Students lose motivation if they don't know *why* they are doing something and if they are given too long to do a task. Showing pupils that they have made progress throughout the lesson is a great way of gaining and keeping motivation. This is why the plenary matters!

Don't wait right until the end of the lesson to review learning. If you do, you run the risk of finding out that learning hasn't been effective and are unable to intervene to resolve things. In outstanding lessons, teachers review and question pupils periodically *throughout* the session to see:

- How are they finding the lesson?
- Is it too easy, too hard, or does it have just the right amount of challenge?
- What have pupils grasped? What do they know? What parts need clarifying?

As Einstein said: *'If you can't explain it simply, you don't understand it well enough.'*

# Mini plenaries

Mini plenaries let pupils think about and show what they have been learning. They break up the lesson and provide crucial information for teachers. Keep them short, fun and inclusive to inject energy into the lesson and keep people on their toes. Try the following:

- Twitter limits messages to 140 characters. Ask pupils to 'tweet' a summary of the lesson so far in written or electronic form. The brevity of the message makes this challenging and helps them distil the most important points. Are they the points you expected to see?

- Ask pupils which of the learning objectives they think they have met so far. Ask them to prove it – in any way, in two minutes!

- Students create a graphic summary of the lesson and what they have learnt so far, eg a flow chart, diagram, steps or other visual representation. What gaps need filling next?

- Pair – Share – Are we there? Ask some questions focused on what they have learnt so far. Students discuss in pairs and respond with their answers. Mini white boards can be used to display answers, letting you see all their responses

# Plenary ideas for lesson ends

Lesson endings are where you want to wrap things up and check pupils' overall progress. A good final plenary helps the class celebrate what they have learnt, but should also signpost the next steps for future lessons.

- Give students a summary of what has been covered in the lesson, but leave out the key words. Pupils must fit these in the correct place

- Key Terms Splat! Display all the key words from the lesson on the board. In pairs, pupils devise a question whose answer will be one of the key terms. Divide the class into two teams. Each team puts forward a person armed with a fly swatter. A series of questions about the topic is now asked (each pair taking it in turn to pose the question they devised). The team representatives swat the term they think is correct. The team with most correctly swatted answers wins the game!

# Plenary ideas for lesson ends

- Pupils hold up the fingers on one hand to show their confidence with a piece of work or idea. They allocate a 5 if they think they are very secure, through to a 1 if they lack knowledge or confidence about it. Pupils need to explain their judgement, sharing good ideas, and time must be spent on any misconceptions – perhaps by asking other more highly-scoring pupils to explain their ideas

- Get pupils using colour to help them summarise learning. One class wrote summaries of the key learning points from the lesson in green in their books. It helped them easily spot and revise the key points for exams

- Challenge pupils to spot and solve the error in a piece of work

- Ask a pupil in the lesson to give a number between 5 and 15. If they say '8', they need to summarise the main things they have learnt in the lesson in only eight words, then share their response with a partner: challenging and fun!

# Plenary ideas for lesson ends

- Get pupils to design a quick three questions related to the topic with their partner. They write the questions on a piece of paper, screw it into a ball and throw it to another pair. Pairs answer the questions and these are shared with the class who check that they are correct

# Effective group work

Great group work is key for building outstanding lessons. It helps pupils stay motivated and interested because it is active. It also builds a range of important 'softer skills' including: co-operation, speaking and listening skills, managing time, independence, etc.

When designed effectively, group work can provide essential differentiation. Pupils can be grouped according to interest, with appropriate work – or when pupils are working in a mixed ability context they can be given different roles and responsibilities within the group. This helps to provide the appropriate level of challenge for all pupils.

Key characteristics of effective group work include:

- Clear instructions (see pages 86 and 87) for a reminder of the key points
- Number of students in a group – ideally no more than four
- Chunking it – give shorter specific tasks and don't expect students to work too long at something without you monitoring and re-focusing them. Build in mini plenaries to check everyone is on task

# Great group work tips

- **Supervision is key**. We all know the tendency to drift off task if we think the 'teacher'/boss isn't watching us, and it is just the same for pupils. Circulating, facing the class and scanning is the best way to ensure that all pupils are on task. Beware the tendency to get so involved with one group that you turn your back to the others

- **Think before asking**. Pupils tend to ask the teacher to solve their queries too quickly. Promote better pupil independence by setting up strategies for them to use before asking you, eg: using displays, reference books, looking again at the exemplar materials, asking their partner. Often a bit of thought by pupils will resolve the problem and ensure that you don't have a massive queue of pupils trailing behind you!

- **Select the groups**. Students need to be able to work with a range of other people, so don't always let them select their own groups. Mix it up, forming groups according to various criteria as appropriate for the lesson

# Different group work strategies

## Pair, share, explain and challenge

We know that really effective lessons employ a range of teaching techniques. Sometimes paired work is the best way to get all pupils fully engaged. It's a great way to manage a boisterous class that easily gets 'off task' in bigger groups.

To get pupils interacting with other class members, ask them to reflect, explain or explore something with a partner, then turn around and feed back to another person. This way you stage the group work and remain in control.

Swapping pairs like this can increase the challenge, particularly if the second person has to quiz, use a checklist or challenge the initial response. Pupils are forced to review their work in the light of another person's comments and feed back their response on their own (away from their initial partner). This creates greater autonomy.

Students who don't feel that they get their share of 'air time' in a lesson can become noisy. Another benefit of this approach is that it gives *all* pupils a voice.

# Different group work strategies

## Jigsaw

If you are allowing pupils to work in larger groups, then one good way of ensuring a high level of response is to give different groups a separate area to look at. Another idea is to give them contrasting resources to work on.

1.  Explain to pupils that different groups have been given the responsibility to work on different, specified areas of a topic. Make it clear to pupils that each individual in that group will be expected later in the lesson to share their findings with a new group. (This creates the motivation for pupils to work particularly hard as they know their understanding will be tested later on).

2.  Give pupils a clear allotted time scale for their group work. This helps keep them focused and gives urgency to the task.

3.  As the allocated time for the group task draws to a close, remind pupils that they will have to share their findings with people from all different groups. Give each person on the table a number. Then re-group the students, so that members from different groups are on tables together.

# Different group work strategies

## Jigsaw

4.  Specify the amount of time available for each pupil to feed back their key findings to the other people on their new table. This leads to a good exchange of information. Since all pupils are engaged in feeding back their findings, this is an effective way of ensuring pupil motivation as it promotes individual responsibility. It also avoids long tedious feedback sessions focused on just a few pupils contributing their ideas through the teacher.

5.  At the end of the session – you might want to draw together some of the key findings from each area, and use further questions to tease out and clarify any important points.

**CASE STUDY**

*In a History investigation each group was given different sources, (written texts, copies of documents, pictures) relating to the death of Charles I. Each group discussed what they found out about the incident from their source and then shared that information with people from different tables. In the plenary the different interpretations of the incident were discussed, highlighting the issue of bias. Everyone was involved and engaged and everyone took some ownership of the task.*

# Make them think

Posing questions, setting challenges and getting pupils to think about what the purpose of a task should be – all of these develop and hone students' critical thinking skills. They guard against creating pupil dependency, a trap we fall into if we step in too quickly to help a pupil. When thinking about your lessons, consider:

*   How hard have you made pupils think today?
*   What different strategies have you used to get all pupils engaged in higher level thinking skills?

A great plenary idea is to give the pupils the key words and ask them to think of the question. It sounds easy but is harder than you think. Take these words from a recent science lesson – *photosynthesis, light, oxygen, released, carbohydrates*. Now devise the question. I am sure that got you thinking!

The questions that students come up with take a lot of thought (more than is often required in answering some questions in some lessons) and are really useful in helping you see how they've made sense of the lesson.

# Promote high-level thinking

Outstanding teachers develop thinking skills by:

- Providing several answers or solutions and asking pupils to discuss which is right
- Creating and encouraging debate
- Asking students for their ideas about **how** they will best learn something
- Asking students to design or lead aspects of the lesson such as feeding back on each other's work or designing a plenary
- Having lessons where pupils do not write down things but are instead asked to reflect on and discuss the thought processes involved. *A high ability Maths class regularly has 'no writing' lessons where pupils are set high level problems and puzzles. They have to think about them, and solve them by discussion alone.*

Lots of note-making or copying from the board can makes pupils look busy, but that doesn't mean they are having a deep learning experience. Why not ask them to present an idea as a diagram or summarise it in just ten words? Sometimes getting them to think more, but write less is important.

# Taking risks and embracing failure

To teach outstanding lessons you need a frequent injection of innovation and good ideas. It might feel risky suddenly to experiment or try out something new with a class, but this approach keeps things fresh and does lead to better lessons.

Exciting and creative ideas come from other staff and by adapting material. The TES website, www.tes.co.uk  offers a host of free subject-specific teaching ideas, including 3,500 Teachers TV videos. Watching somebody else have a go, even when they aren't always successful, can be a great way of learning new ideas.

Accomplished teachers create a culture in their classes where pupils know that some failure is to be expected. If students don't feel that they can have a go, and make a mistake this will hinder their learning. They will be hesitant, unwilling to accept challenges and they will fail to make good progress. We need to make them feel confident that good learning is about taking risks, sometimes failing, but always learning from our mistakes:

*'When we get it wrong, it is not bad – it's because we are learning!'* **Year 5 pupil**.

# Why failure leads to better learning

> 'Anyone who has never made a mistake has never tried anything new.' **Einstein**

If we adopt a positive mind-set in our own approach to teaching lessons and encourage pupils not to fear failure, we should also model it for our classes. We should not be afraid to trial new ideas and experiment with teaching techniques. Being aware of the 'implementation dip' involved in trying out new things will help encourage experimentation and this can result in much better lessons.

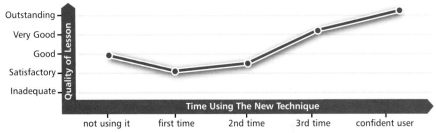

The graph shows that the first time you try a new technique your lesson quality may well decrease. However, once you become a confident user and your class understands the technique your lessons will improve.

# Learning challenging things

**True story:**

One Head of Department spoke to me about teaching weaker students: 'I've told staff to make things really basic: don't try and teach them the term 'pipette', just tell them it is a 'dropper'.'

This approach won't lead to challenging lessons or exceptional progress. A real sign of excellence is a lesson where all pupils are challenged and the teacher expects the best from every student. Motivate children to want to learn difficult things by:

- Praising them and preparing them for the challenge – *'I'm teaching you this; it's tricky, but you can do it... and I'm going to show you how.'*
- Explaining key vocabulary, and teaching strategies to learn it and spell it correctly
- Using displays and referring to them to consolidate new vocabulary or terms
- Pointing out the different strategies *you* have for learning things and getting pupils to experiment with these themselves
- Modelling good practice – you don't have to be amazing at all aspects of the subject yourself, but you can show pupils how to overcome challenges by checking their work, revising first drafts or learning key terms

# Behaviour

Pupil behaviour is very well managed in outstanding lessons and pupils are motivated to do well. (See *Behaviour Management Pocketbook* and *Challenging Behaviours Pocketbook* for more detailed coverage of this huge area). Good teachers know that they can't make pupils behave but they can influence them and set up conditions and expectations to make good behaviour more likely. They are aware of the importance of:

- **The learning climate and classroom environment**. Well organised and well cared for environments and resources promote high expectations

- **How they speak to and act towards their students**. Pupils soon detect teachers who are bored/ tired/ uninterested or timid. Accomplished teachers act positively and with enthusiasm, even when they least feel like it. How they talk and act sets the tone of the lesson

- **Well planned and engaging lessons** involving a range of teaching strategies with a good level of pace and challenge

# Motivate pupils to behave better

In highly successful lessons teachers motivate pupils by creating a positive climate in which effective learning takes place:

- They make sure that *all* pupils feel safe, secure and valued. Pupils can't learn effectively if they are scared, stressed or belittled by their peers or teacher
- They understand that when pupils ask or answer a question they are taking a risk. They show that they value students' contributions, whether their answers are right or wrong
- They show approval and appreciation of students, encouraging them to participate, and offering plenty of praise. (A good guide is to aim for a minimum of three positive comments to each negative comment.)
- They are positive and show that they are excited by and appreciate teaching their students. Students notice this and reciprocate

Outstanding lessons really are based on developing great relationships with others and all our interactions influence this.

# Identify the alpha

In all groups there are key players. Teaching in over 80 schools, I have found that if I notice and get these individuals 'on side' then the class will behave and the lesson will succeed.

'Alphas' or 'influencers' are those pupils that the group looks to when deciding how to react to things. If the alphas approve, *they* do; if the alphas behave, *they* will; if the alphas think the task is worth bothering with, *they* will. But if the alphas don't, then the whole class can misbehave.

Typical alphas are dominant individuals – often boisterous males, but sometimes a popular girl or a witty, quieter individual. What is important is that their reactions can sway the whole class. Tap into this to motivate the whole group.

**Getting them on side is not**: letting them get away with things/letting them rule the roost. **It is**: noticing them (they often use misbehaviour as a way of gaining attention). Try to praise them in the first few minutes of the lesson. Use their name and, if relevant, give them a role or responsibility so they have an investment in the lesson being successful.

# You can influence behaviour

Pupils *like* well ordered classrooms where they can focus and concentrate. They need teachers to be firm, clear and fair. They want us to set boundaries and keep good order. Students made the following comments about teachers who manage classrooms effectively:

- *'We know what Miss wants us to do.'*
- *'We get lots of praise for good work and trying hard.'*
- *'We take it in turns to be monitors (for books etc) and get merits for this.'*
- *'We enjoy lessons. They are interesting – we want to take part in the activities.'*

Our behaviour, our motivation and our attitude towards our students influences *their* behaviour and *their* motivation which is so important in teaching outstanding lessons.

# Pupils quickly spot an ineffective teacher

We can also pick up some useful hints from pupils about where some teachers are going wrong. They made the following comments about staff who were less effective in maintaining good order and in motivating their classes:

- *'Miss is just too timid and sheepish. I think she's scared to tell us off.'* (Unassertive)
- *'He isn't fair! Other people were talking too, he just picks on me.'* (Unjust)
- *'It's hard to know where you are with him: sometimes he's chilled, other times he gets stressed about the very same thing!'* (Unpredictable and inconsistent)

What might my pupils say about me?

What would I like them to say about me?

What techniques can I use to ensure this happens?

Myth vs Reality

 Developing Great Relationships

 Planning Outstanding Lessons

 It's About Them – Not You!

 The X Factor

 Resources and Techniques

 Motivate 'em!

 Moving Forward

# Moving Forward

# Evaluating your successes

Teaching outstanding lessons requires skill and judgement. Reflecting on and learning from your failures as well as your successes is the way to sharpen your skills. A simple way to improve your practice is to audit your strengths and areas for development:

- Ask observers for feedback on your practice. Why not ask a friend to watch your lesson? What appears to be helping your students to learn? What could be better?
- Look at your students' work and test scores. Is there evidence of good progress?
- Ask students for their views on your lessons. What do they find useful? What could be improved?
- Watch somebody else teach a topic or class you find challenging – can you learn anything from their skills?

> 'When teachers seek, or are at least open to, feedback from students as to what students know, what they understand, where they make errors, when they have misconceptions, when they are not engaged – then teaching and learning can be synchronized and powerful. Feedback to teachers helps make learning visible.'
> **Visible Learning** by John Hattie

# See what they see

Watching a video of yourself teaching allows you to see yourself as your pupils see you. It is a very powerful way of improving practice. It highlights your teaching strengths and weaknesses.

Consider videoing yourself teaching one of your classes, (but check with your headteacher first, so that any necessary permission is obtained). When you observe yourself, consider:

- **How well the pupils respond to the lesson**. Are *all* pupils included and motivated? Are there any groups or individuals that are less engaged?
- **How you respond and speak to the pupils**. Are your explanations clear? Do you include all pupils? Are you making good eye contact with all pupils? What appears to help them learn? What could be better?

1. Make a note of the best things you observe. Celebrate these!
2. Identify a couple of areas for improvement and think about what you will do to improve your practice here. Keep it clear and simple to implement – and don't forget to review it.

# Self-audit

On the following page are some aspects of outstanding lessons. Have a look at each one and consider how effectively you feel these are happening in your lessons:

**(1)** Never – this is not part of my current practice.

**(2)** Sometimes – occasionally these things happen in my lessons.

**(3)** Frequently – this is often part of my regular classroom practice.

**(4)** Mastered – this reflects my current practice and it has a positive effect in the classroom.

Look at the areas you feel secure about. Next consider those that you feel are less developed. This will help pinpoint areas for development and will help you set some targets.

# Self-audit

| Some Features of Outstanding Lessons | Current Practice |
|---|---|
| All pupils are actively engaged in the lesson. The teacher uses her subject knowledge to inspire pupils. Resources and teaching techniques are relevant, engaging and well suited to the learning objective. | ① ② ③ ④ |
| By the end of the lesson, the learning gains are clear and pupils can comment on what progress they have made. | ① ② ③ ④ |
| Teachers systematically check learning throughout the lesson, through expert questioning and other strategies. | ① ② ③ ④ |
| A high level of challenge and expectation is set in lessons. Pupils are not afraid to try appropriately challenging tasks. | ① ② ③ ④ |
| Pupils know their target grade or level. | ① ② ③ ④ |
| Pupils can explain what they need to do to reach their next levels. They understand their next steps in learning. | ① ② ③ ④ |
| Pupil motivation and behaviour are very good. They work very well in a range of group, pair and individual settings. Any misbehaviour is managed effectively by the teacher, so that it does not have an adverse impact on others. | ① ② ③ ④ |
| Teaching assistants and other staff provide support clearly targeted at individual need. Any support promotes pupil independence, rather than dependence. | ① ② ③ ④ |
| Pupils make excellent progress in the lesson. It is clear that excellent learning gains have been made by all. Pupils' work shows very good progress across time. | ① ② ③ ④ |

# Choosing an area to develop and seeking inspiration

When you have identified an area you would like to develop, think about how you will enable this to happen. Look for inspiration in your school or college. Find out from students and other teachers:

- Who does this well?
- What different strategies do other teachers have for making this happen?
- Where can I see good practice?

Don't be afraid to ask other people to share ideas or to let you observe their classes. Most people don't mind sharing because you are showing your admiration for their skills. To get a wider perspective seek views from teachers in different schools, (or even countries) by researching an issue, watching a video or reading a book that considers this area in detail.

Try 'YouTube' for some clips on innovative practice and follow lead educators on Twitter. One huge benefit of Twitter is that following one person/organisation readily links you to snippets of other good ideas, research and practice.

# Still seeking inspiration?

- Look at published research at www.oftsed.gov.uk, www.suttontrust.com as well as university research

- Most specific subjects have subject associations that review effective ideas and publications. These can inspire and save you time! Subject associations are listed on this site: www.subjectassociation.org.uk

- The TES website (www.tes.co.uk) – thousands of free subject-specific teaching ideas, lesson resources, and *Teachers' TV* videos

- Look at the reviews of the latest teaching books on Amazon – many schools are starting staff libraries to share good books and ideas for teaching resources. See the back of the book for my current favourites

# Being observed

You are likely to have your lessons observed by a range of people for different reasons. Lesson observation in all its guises is covered more fully in the *Lesson Observation Pocketbook*, but the following pages provide advice within the context of outstanding lessons. When being observed:

1. Have a plan but don't be afraid to adapt and amend it in the light of pupils' responses.
2. Focus on the pupils: how are they learning? Are they engaged?
3. Recap and review mid-way through the lesson to check progress and re-focus pupils.
4. Involve pupils in the lesson – we learn more by doing than just listening.
5. Reflect and ask for feedback: from pupils, as well as from observers. Ask what worked well, but also be prepared to take feedback about what could be better.

Teaching isn't an exact science: we can all learn and improve!

# What observers look for

Observers consider a range of aspects when they watch a lesson:

- The basics – obviously some things are absolutely essential such as pupil safety, and an appropriate use of equipment. But atmosphere and environment are also important

- How does the teacher use the environment to motivate students? How effective are the displays? Are resources well suited for the specific purpose of that lesson and are they relevant for all the pupils' abilities? Are there sufficient for everybody to become engaged and independent or are lots of students sharing resources?

- What would it be like to be a pupil in this class? How would I feel? How does the teacher interact with the class? Does she encourage everybody? Do I feel inspired and motivated to give of my best? Do all of the students get involved? Does the teacher encourage and challenge everybody?

# What observers look for in outstanding lessons

- How does the lesson progress the pupils' learning? This is absolutely key. If students spend an hour in a lesson what have they gained from it? What skills have they learnt? Or what are they better able to do? In outstanding lessons pupils make exceptional progress. Often this is because the teacher has the highest expectations of the class and encourages and pushes them to think further for themselves. An outstanding teacher doesn't accept the first answer; they keep on challenging

- Pupil independence. In excellent lessons the teacher is the facilitator, encouraging students to develop their skills, to explore and find out things for themselves. The students usually speak much more than the teacher and there is good interaction among all class members

# Examples from outstanding lessons

Look at these notes from an observer's notebook on two outstanding lessons. Consider their chief characteristics:

> ### Lesson 1
> 'A firm start to the lesson – business-like approach and excellent pace to challenge and motivate the group. Clear and well-structured questions to push students further. High expectations, efficient use of resources, sound subject knowledge...'
>
> ### Lesson 2
> 'Good use of questioning to gauge understanding. Skilful interventions to draw attention to developments and encourage focused analysis. Good maintenance of pace and high expectations. Excellent sharing of exam technique...'

Notice how the observer has picked out the strengths. Both lessons show good progress and teacher subject knowledge. They focus on challenge and high expectations *by* the teacher *for* the students.

# Good practice

Observers should share their observation criteria with you before the observation. Ofsted's specific criteria, for instance, can be found on their website: www.ofsted.gov.uk. If you are being observed by a colleague, it can be helpful to agree a focus for the observation, eg 'use of questioning', or 'pupil engagement'.

Good observers and inspectors give feedback soon after the lesson when it is still fresh in the assessor's and teacher's mind. If you receive a judgement such as 'good' or 'satisfactory' the observer needs to tell you what you would have needed to do to make it the next level. It is important that clear areas for improvement are identified so you know what you should be focusing on.

Hearing other people's reviews of your lessons should be a positive experience, a way of receiving feedback about what you do well and what could be even better.

# In summary

Teaching is an exciting and dynamic profession. By reflecting on your own practice you will develop the skills to transform ordinary lessons into outstanding learning experiences.

Remember, teaching outstanding lessons depends upon your interactions with your pupils, how you help them learn and how much progress they make. It's developing a balance between building great relationships and making outstanding learning experiences happen. By planning well-thought-out, challenging and stimulating lessons and nurturing a positive classroom climate, you can ensure that you encourage pupils so that they feel enthused and excited about learning:

> 'A teacher affects eternity; he can never tell where his influence stops.'
> **Henry Brooks Adams, American Historian**

# Further reading

*Assessment & Learning Pocketbook* by Ian Smith.
Published by Teachers' Pocketbooks, 2007

*Assessment for Learning: Why, What and How?* by Dylan Wiliam.
Published by Institute of Education, 2009

*Assessment for Learning: Putting it into Practice* by Paul Black et al.
Published by Open University Press, 2003

*Behaviour Management Pocketbook (2nd edition)* by Peter Hook and Andy Vass.
Published by Teachers' Pocketbooks, 2011

*Formative Assessment in the Secondary Classroom* by Shirley Clarke.
Published by Hodder Education, 2005

*How to be an Amazing Teacher* by Caroline Bentley-Davies.
Published by Crown House, 2010

*The Lazy Teacher's Handbook* by Jim Smith.
Published by Crown House, 2010

*Lesson Observation Pocketbook* by Roy Watson-Davies.
Published by Teachers' Pocketbooks, 2009

*Visible Learning* by John Hattie.
Published by Routledge, 2008

# About the author

**Caroline Bentley-Davies**

Caroline is an Oxford graduate who started teaching in the mid-1990s. She has been a middle leader in three schools, an Education Adviser for a Local Authority and an educational consultant across the UK and overseas.

Over a five-year period she has run demonstration lessons in over 80 schools. Caroline runs training sessions for teachers focusing on the skills of an outstanding teacher, assessment for learning strategies, motivating and improving pupil behaviour. Her reputation means that she has been invited to speak in schools from Dubai to Denmark. She has trained teachers from the United States to Russia.

For information about her training, consultancy and other books please see Caroline's website: www.bentley-davies.co.uk or follow her on twitter @Real CBD.

Caroline runs a range of training courses hosted by Osiris Education (www.OsirisEducational.co.uk) as well as training days directly with individual schools.

# Order form

## Your details

Name _____

Position _____

School _____

Address _____

_____

_____

Telephone _____

Fax _____

E-mail _____

VAT No. (EC only) _____

Your Order Ref _____

## Please send me:

No.
copies

Outstanding Lessons _____ Pocketbook ☐

_____ Pocketbook ☐

_____ Pocketbook ☐

_____ Pocketbook ☐

**Order by Post**

## Teachers' Pocketbooks

Laurel House, Station Approach
Alresford, Hants. SO24 9JH UK

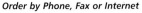

**Order by Phone, Fax or Internet**

Telephone: +44 (0)1962 735573
Facsimile: +44 (0)1962 733637
Email: sales@teacherspocketbooks.co.uk
Web: www.teacherspocketbooks.co.uk

**Customers in USA should contact:**

2427 Bond Street, University Park, IL 60466
Tel: 866 620 6944   Facsimile: 708 534 7803
Email: mp.orders@ware-pak.com
Web: www.managementpocketbooks.com